Symbols, Landmarks, and Monuments

Independence Hall

Tamara L. Britton
ABDO Publishing Company

visit us at
www.abdopub.com

Published by ABDO Publishing Company, 4940 Viking Drive, Edina, Minnesota 55435.
Copyright © 2003 by Abdo Consulting Group, Inc. International copyrights reserved in all countries. No part of this book may be reproduced in any form without written permission from the publisher.

Printed in the United States of America

Editors: Kate A. Conley, Kristy Langanki Cannon, Kristianne E. Vieregger
Photo Credits: AP/Wide World, Corbis
Art Direction & Maps: Neil Klinepier

Library of Congress Cataloging-in-Publication Data

Britton, Tamara L., 1963-
    Independence Hall / Tamara L. Britton.
       p. cm. -- (Symbols, landmarks, and monuments)
    Includes index.
    Summary: Explores the history of the Pennsylvania State House, later called Independence Hall, where the Declaration of Independence and Articles of Confederation were adopted and the Constitution was signed.
    ISBN 1-57765-853-1
    1. Independence Hall (Philadelphia, Pa.)--Juvenile literature. 2. Philadelphia (Pa.)--Buildings, structures, etc.--Juvenile literature. 3. United States--Politics and government--1775-1783--Juvenile literature. 4. United States--Politics and government--1783-1789--Juvenile literature. [1. Independence Hall (Philadelphia, Pa.) 2. Philadelphia (Pa.)--Buildings, structures, etc. 3. United States--Politics and government--1775-1783. 4. United States--Politics and government--1783-1789.] I. Title

F158.8.I3 B63 2002
974.8'11--dc21
                                                              2002066670

Contents

Independence Hall

A walk down Chestnut Street in Philadelphia, Pennsylvania, is like a walk through a U.S. history book. That is where, among other historic buildings, the red-brick Pennsylvania State House stands. Many important events that led to the nation's founding occurred there.

Today, Washington, D.C., is the capital of the United States. But earlier in U.S. history, America's leaders met in Philadelphia. So Philadelphia is home to many important **landmarks**, monuments, and historic events.

The First and Second Continental **Congresses** met in Philadelphia. There, in the Pennsylvania State House, the **Founding Fathers** adopted the

Independence Hall is in the heart of Philadelphia, Pennsylvania.

Declaration of Independence. **Congress** members agreed on the Articles of Confederation. They discussed, wrote, and signed the U.S. **Constitution** at the Pennsylvania State House, too.

For these reasons, Philadelphia is often called the birthplace of the United States. Because of all the important events in America's early history that happened there, the Pennsylvania State House is now called Independence Hall.

The historic State House was an important setting in America's struggle for independence.

Fun Facts

√ Independence Hall's basement once served as Philadelphia's dog pound.

√ The design of the American flag was agreed upon in Independence Hall.

√ Artist Charles Willson Peale rented Independence Hall for $400 a year.

√ The 2,000-pound (907-kg) Liberty Bell is made from copper and tin, with small amounts of lead, zinc, arsenic, and gold.

√ The final ring of the Liberty Bell was on George Washington's birthday in 1846.

√ Independence National Historical Park was designated a World Heritage Site in 1979.

√ The inkstand that the signers of the Declaration of Independence used is still in Independence Hall.

√ The Rising Sun Chair still stands in Independence Hall. It was where George Washington sat when he presided over the Constitutional Convention.

Timeline

1681 √ King Charles II gives land to William Penn. It becomes the Pennsylvania Colony.

1729 √ Pennsylvania's assembly works toward the design and construction of a permanent meeting place.

1735 √ Pennsylvania's assembly begins meeting on the first floor of the new Pennsylvania State House.

1753 √ Construction on the State House is finally completed.

1776 √ On July 4, the Second Continental Congress approves the Declaration of Independence at the State House.

1781 √ The Second Continental Congress ratifies the Articles of Confederation at the State House.

1787 √ The Congress of the Confederation signs the U.S. Constitution at the State House.

1799 √ Pennsylvania's government moves to Lancaster, Pennsylvania. The State House stands largely unused.

1802 √ Charles Willson Peale rents the State House and turns it into a museum.

1896 √ The Daughters of the American Revolution begin restoring the State House.

1948 √ The U.S. Congress creates Independence National Historical Park.

Penn's Woods

In 1607, three ships from England landed on present-day Virginia's shores. The men on these ships founded the Virginia Colony. Soon, other people came to America. Many came to work in established colonies. Others came to start new colonies.

King Charles II

In 1681, England's King Charles II gave William Penn land in America. There, Penn started a colony as a home for **Quakers**. He named the colony Sylvania, which means woods. The king added the name Penn to honor Sir William Penn, William Penn's father. He was a respected admiral in the English Navy.

Each colony was under British rule. However, they each had their own laws and government. Penn thought the

William Penn

Pennsylvania colonists should govern themselves. So when he wrote the colony's first **constitution**, he created an **assembly**. And he gave the people religious freedom, property protection, and jury trials.

Pennsylvania's government continued to change. In 1696, the colonists adopted a new constitution, called Markham's Frame. It gave the assembly the power to make laws. In 1701, William Penn **drafted** the Charter of Privileges. It made the assembly independent of the governor. It also allowed the assembly members to meet whenever they wanted.

King Charles II hands William Penn the Pennsylvania charter.

The Pennsylvania State House

Pennsylvania Colony's **assembly** had no official meeting place. So the members met in their homes. In 1729, assembly members decided they needed a permanent meeting place. They chose a location to build a state house.

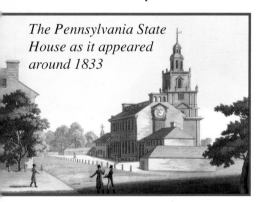

The Pennsylvania State House as it appeared around 1833

The assembly chose **Speaker** Andrew Hamilton to design the building. Hamilton drew the plans. Then he hired master carpenter Edmond Woolley. Woolley was in charge of the state house's construction.

In 1735, the Pennsylvania assembly began meeting on the first floor of the new Pennsylvania State House. In 1748, the second floor was ready to use. The State House was finally complete in 1753 when its **steeple** and bell were installed.

The Pennsylvania State House proved to be a valuable meeting place.

The Liberty Bell

In 1750, **assembly** members decided to honor the fiftieth anniversary of the Charter of Privileges. So they ordered a bell for the State House's **steeple** from England's Whitechapel Foundry.

The new bell arrived in 1752 and was hung in the steeple on March 10, 1753. When the bell was first rung, it cracked! The bell had been too brittle. So assembly members hired John Pass and John Stow to melt it down and recast it.

When Pass and Stow melted the bell, they added copper to strengthen it. Then they recast it. The bell was hung again on March 29. When the bell was rung, assembly members did not like the sound it made.

In 1846, the Liberty Bell cracked again. It has not been rung since.

So Pass and Stow melted and recast the bell again. It was hung again on June 11. Assembly members still did not like the sound the bell made. So they ordered a new one from Whitechapel Foundry.

The new bell did not sound better than the original. However, the new bell was hung in the **cupola** and attached to the clock to toll the hours. The original bell stayed in the **steeple**. This bell is known as the Liberty Bell.

Today, the Liberty Bell is on display for visitors to enjoy.

The First Continental Congress

Though the 13 colonies had their own governments, they were still under British rule. Britain's King George III thought the colonies should help pay for their military. So Britain's **Parliament** began charging the colonists taxes.

The Boston Tea Party was a turning point in American history.

This angered the colonists. They did not think they should pay taxes when they had no representatives in the British **Parliament**. But the Parliament continued to pass tax laws.

The tax laws affected everyday life in the colonies. In 1765, the Stamp Act required colonists to buy tax stamps to put on paper goods. In 1767, the Townshend Acts taxed the paper, glass, paint, and tea that was imported into the colonies.

In Boston, Massachusetts, colonists rebelled against the taxes. On December 16, 1773, colonists boarded ships in the harbor and threw the imported tea on board into the ocean. This is called the Boston Tea Party.

To punish the Boston colonists, Parliament passed the Coercive Acts. These laws closed Boston's harbor. They took away the power of the colonists to elect their council members. They also allowed colonists' trials to be moved to England.

The colonists called the Coercive Acts the Intolerable Acts. They would not tolerate this treatment from Britain's government. So they formed the First Continental **Congress**. It would unite the colonies, represent their interests, and address complaints about the Coercive Acts.

On September 5, 1774, the First Continental **Congress** met in Carpenters' Hall in Philadelphia, Pennsylvania. Twelve colonies sent 56 delegates to the meeting. Georgia was the only colony that did not send any delegates.

At the meeting, the delegates wrote the Declaration of Rights. It said that Americans had certain rights. They were life, liberty, property, **assembly**, and trial by jury. The document demanded that Britain recognize these rights. And it asked Britain to **repeal** many laws, including the Coercive Acts.

The First Continental Congress wanted to work with the king to resolve their differences. So the delegates wrote the Continental Association. It said that the colonies would not buy British goods until the king dealt with their concerns. They hoped the king would want to work together to avoid losing money.

The First Continental **Congress adjourned** on October 26, 1774. The delegates decided to meet again on May 10, 1775, if the king had not addressed their concerns.

Carpenters' Hall

The Second Continental Congress

Relations between Britain and the colonies worsened. The **American Revolution** began in April of 1775. The Second Continental **Congress** met in the Pennsylvania State House that May. The delegates voted to take responsibility for the military. On June 15, they appointed George Washington commander of the Continental Army.

The delegates had many reasons to consider declaring independence from Britain. Britain refused to work with the colonies to settle their differences. The fighting between the king's army and the colonists was bitter. And the king was hiring soldiers from other countries to fight against the colonists.

The delegates decided to separate from Britain and create a new nation. They asked five men to write the Declaration of Independence. Thomas Jefferson did most of the writing.

On July 4, 1776, the Second Continental **Congress** approved the Declaration of Independence. Four days later, the Liberty Bell rang. It called citizens to the State House yard to hear the first public reading of the Declaration of Independence. In the Pennsylvania State House, the 13 colonies became the United States of America.

Continental Congress members Benjamin Franklin, Thomas Jefferson, John Adams, Philip Livingston, and Roger Sherman draft the Declaration of Independence (left). Congress members sign the Declaration of Independence (below).

The Articles of Confederation

The Second Continental **Congress** continued to meet. The delegates worked on a form of government that would unite the states with a central government. But they also wanted the states to have some independence.

On November 15, 1777, the delegates agreed on the Articles of Confederation. The **document** provided for a central government. But it left most power with the states.

The Congress **ratified** the Articles of Confederation in the Pennsylvania State House in 1781. It served as the first U.S. **constitution**. Now, the Congress was called the Congress of the Confederation.

The Conference Room

The Articles of Confederation had flaws. It did not give the central government the power to collect taxes. So the federal government could not pay for its programs. It also had no **judicial** branch to enforce its laws in the states. So in 1787, the **Congress** of the Confederation met to amend the **document**.

The Second Continental Congress met in the Assembly Room.

The U.S. Constitution

The **Congress** of the Confederation met in the Pennsylvania State House in May of 1787. This meeting is called the **Constitutional** Convention. The delegates' goal was to write a constitution that limited the federal government's power. But the federal government also needed to be strong enough to enforce its laws.

So the delegates wrote a constitution that divided the government into **executive**, **legislative**, and **judicial** branches. The branches had a system of **checks and balances**. This limited the government's power and secured the people's liberty.

The U.S. Constitution

The federal government had only the powers stated in the **Constitution**. The states held all the other powers. This was an exciting, new kind of government.

On September 17, 1787, delegates signed the U.S. Constitution in the Pennsylvania State House. On March 4, 1789, the **Congress** of the Confederation ended. Now, the government ruled under the Constitution.

The Declaration of Independence and the U.S. Constitution were both signed in Independence Hall.

New Life for the State House

From 1790 to 1800, Philadelphia was the U.S. capital. The U.S. **Congress** met in the **county** courthouse. Pennsylvania's state government met in the Pennsylvania State House.

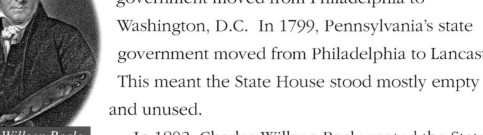
Charles Willson Peale

Soon, however, the situation changed. The U.S. government moved from Philadelphia to Washington, D.C. In 1799, Pennsylvania's state government moved from Philadelphia to Lancaster. This meant the State House stood mostly empty and unused.

In 1802, Charles Willson Peale rented the State House. Peale was a famous painter. He painted portraits of historic figures such as George Washington, Benjamin Franklin, John Adams, and Thomas Jefferson.

Peale also collected natural history specimens. He wanted a place to display his collection. So he made the State House a museum.

In 1812, state officials wanted to build fireproof storage rooms at the State House. So they tore down the State House's wing buildings. This destroyed the library, the committee rooms, and other **architectural** treasures.

Viewing art in the State House

Peale's painting of George Washington

In 1816, the city of Philadelphia bought the State House for $70,000. Officials planned to use it as a city hall. They began remodeling the structure. Workers plastered the inside walls. They removed original woodwork from the **Assembly Room**. And they added a fancier front door.

In 1828, city officials ordered a new **steeple**. In 1831, they began restoring the Assembly Room. The Liberty Bell was removed from the steeple in 1852. It was put in the Assembly Room. This further changed the building's original design.

In 1896, the **Daughters of the American Revolution** wanted to restore the State House to its original beauty. They hired an **architect** to plan the restoration.

During the restoration, workers tore down the storage rooms that had been added in 1812. And they built wing buildings like the originals. Public support for restoring historic buildings such as the State House grew into the next century.

The restored Supreme Court Chamber

The National Park

After the country's success in **World War II**, Americans became more **patriotic**. Many wanted to preserve places important to the nation's history. So in 1948, the U.S. **Congress** created Independence National Historical Park in Philadelphia. It is part of the National Park system. Independence Hall is located within the park's four-block Independence Square area.

The **county** courthouse is in the park, too. The U.S. Congress met there when Philadelphia was the nation's capital. It is where the first two U.S. presidents were **inaugurated**. Today, the courthouse is known as Congress Hall.

Also located in the park is Carpenters' Hall, where the First Continental Congress met. The First and Second Banks of the United States are in the park, too. These banks helped form the new nation's banking system. Also in the park are historic houses and museums.

Many important events in U.S. history leading to independence happened in the Pennsylvania State House. That is why the State House is now called Independence Hall. Independence Hall and the other buildings in Independence National Historical Park are some of America's most important national monuments.

Independence National Historical Park

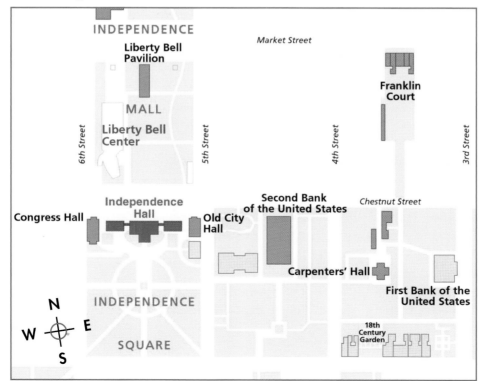

Glossary

adjourn - to stop work until a later time.

American Revolution - 1775 to 1783. A war for independence between Britain and its North American colonies. The colonists won and created the United States.

architecture - the style of a building.

assembly - a group of government officials who make and discuss laws.

checks and balances - a term used to describe the relationship between the three branches of government in the United States. No branch has power over the others. So no single group can control the country.

Congress - a formal meeting of delegates for discussion and usually action on some question. Today, the U.S. Congress is the lawmaking body of the United States. It is made up of the Senate and the House of Representatives. It meets in Washington, D.C.

constitution - the laws that govern a colony or a country. The U.S. Constitution contains the laws that govern the United States.

county - the largest local government within a state.

cupola - a dome-shaped structure built on the rooftop of a building.

Daughters of the American Revolution - an organization of women who are descendants of those who served or aided in the American Revolution. The organization promotes historical, patriotic, and educational activities.

document - an official paper.

draft - to compose or prepare.

executive - the branch of a government that puts laws into effect.

Founding Fathers - the leading figures in the founding of the United States.

inaugurate - to be sworn into a political office.

judicial - the branch of a government that administers the laws.

landmark - an important structure of historical or physical importance.

legislative - the branch of a government that makes laws.

parliament - the highest lawmaking body of some governments.

patriotic - showing love and support for one's country.

Quaker - a member of the religious group called the Society of Friends.

ratify - to officially approve.

repeal - to formally withdraw or cancel.

speaker - a person who is part of an assembly.

steeple - a tall tower with a spire on top, built on the rooftop of a building.

World War II - 1939 to 1945, fought in Europe, Asia, and Africa. The United States, France, Great Britain, the Soviet Union, and their allies were on one side. Germany, Italy, Japan, and their allies were on the other side. The war began when Germany invaded Poland. The United States entered the war in 1941 after Japan bombed Pearl Harbor, Hawaii.

Web Sites

Would you like to learn more about Independence Hall? Please visit **www.abdopub.com** to find up-to-date Web site links about Independence Hall's history and Independence National Historical Park. These links are routinely monitored and updated to provide the most current information available.

Index